Home Office Research Study 238

Tackling racial equality: international comparisons

Mary Coussey

The views expressed in this report are those of the authors, not necessarily those of the Home Office (nor do they reflect Government policy).

Home Office Research, Development and Statistics Directorate
April 2002

Home Office Research Studies

The Home Office Research Studies are reports on research undertaken by or on behalf of the Home Office. They cover the range of subjects for which the Home Secretary has responsibility. Other publications produced by the Research, Development and Statistics Directorate include Findings, Statistical Bulletins and Statistical Papers.

The Research, Development and Statistics Directorate

RDS is part of the Home Office. The Home Office's purpose is to build a safe, just and tolerant society in which the rights and responsibilities of individuals, families and communities are properly balanced and the protection and security of the public are maintained.

RDS is also part of National Statistics (NS). One of the aims of NS is to inform Parliament and the citizen about the state of the nation and provide a window on the work and performance of government, allowing the impact of government policies and actions to be assessed.

Therefore –

Research Development and Statistics Directorate exists to improve policy making, decision taking and practice in support of the Home Office purpose and aims, to provide the public and Parliament with information necessary for informed debate and to publish information for future use.

First published 2002
Application for reproduction should be made to the Communication Development Unit, Room 201, Home Office, 50 Queen Anne's Gate, London SW1H 9AT.
© Crown copyright 2002   ISBN   1 84082 805 6
ISSN   0072 6435

Foreword

Earlier this year, governments from across the globe gathered in Durban, South Africa, for the United Nations World Conference Against Racism. The conference was an indication of the scale of the problem of racial discrimination and the level of commitment which exists to tackle it.

There is clearly a wealth of knowledge, experience and good practice to be drawn from the work going on at an international level in this field. We have attempted for the first time to bring that information together into one document.

The aim of this research is to determine how UK policies and programmes compare with those in other countries. Comparing information has been inevitably problematic. There is a significant lack of comparable statistics and an inconsistency in the terms used to define people of immigrant origin and minority communities. However, this paper is a good basis upon which to build and develop our knowledge base. It should be of interest to policy makers and non-governmental organisations both at home and abroad.

Julie Clouder
Head of European and International Unit
Home Office Race Equality Unit

Contents

List of tables

Executive summary

This paper gives an overview of governments' approaches to racial equality in various countries with racially or ethnically diverse populations. These include some European Union (EU) member states, and countries with active policies and programmes, the USA, Canada, Australia and South Africa.[1]

The areas considered are legal measures to combat racial discrimination, to combat hate crimes, racist speech and intolerance, and government activities designed to promote the benefits of tolerance and ethnic diversity.

The countries included in the paper have become racially diverse in different ways, some more recently than others, and have different legal, civil and economic circumstances. This is partly reflected in the different terminology used. In general, those with long-standing ethnically diverse populations have tended to use terms such as 'ethnic minorities' or 'minorities'. Other countries use terms which reflect a more recent experience of immigration, such as 'immigrant' and 'foreigner'. This paper's concern is with measures to protect and improve the position of the visible population who are the victims of racism and racial discrimination, whether or not they are of immigrant origin.

The victims of racial discrimination and intolerance

In all countries referred to in this comparison, except for South Africa, the racially or ethnically visible population which is the main victim of discrimination is in a minority. In EU member states, ethnic minorities came originally as migrant labour, sometimes with temporary status, in the early 1960s and 1970s to the Netherlands, Germany, France and Belgium, from countries such as Morocco, Turkey, and Algeria. In Great Britain, France and the Netherlands immigrants came from former colonies. More recently, Sweden, Denmark, Portugal, Spain and Italy have been receiving immigrants.

Immigrants largely founded the USA, Canada and Australia, two and three centuries ago from Europe and more recently from Asia and, in the USA, Latin America. The USA's African-American population descended from slavery. The majority of South Africa's diverse population is African, with minorities of European, Indian and Malaysian origin, but the white minority has a dominant socio-economic position.

---

1. The material in this paper was drawn from published sources in August 2001, and it does not include developments since then.

Achieving Racial Equality

This paper is confined to legal and other government measures to secure racial equality and to promote diversity. However, it is important to recognise that although governments have a key role in laying the legal and policy foundations for racial equality, and can help promote tolerance, all the other institutions in civil society have an important contribution to make. Although these institutions too have to remove the barriers to full participation, and take action to promote racial equality in their functions and services, their activities are not included.

Legal measures to combat racial discrimination

There are two main approaches to legislation against racial discrimination in European countries. Some like the UK and the Netherlands have specific civil legislation against racial discrimination. Other countries, such as France, Italy, and Portugal, have specific provisions in the criminal code. The use of the criminal code means a higher standard of proof is required than in civil offences to establish racial discrimination. The other main approach is to have a general constitutional provision against racial discrimination, as in Austria, Germany, Spain, and Italy. Several countries have a mixture of specific civil and criminal instruments, and also general constitutional provisions.

The legislation in Great Britain and the Netherlands also covers indirect discrimination and allows affirmative or positive action in employment to help reduce under-representation of ethnic minorities in the workplace. In Great Britain, the government is currently consulting on a scheme giving public authorities a duty to promote racial equality in their functions. Employers in the Netherlands are also required to monitor the proportion of ethnic minorities in their workforce, and have plans to promote proportional representation.

The EU Council Directive 2000 requires member states to enact provisions by 2003 to prevent direct and indirect racial discrimination in employment, occupation, access to training, and other areas. The directive allows positive action to compensate for racially or ethnically-linked disadvantages and requires member states to have adequate support for victims and to designate a specialist body to promote equal treatment and monitor levels of discrimination. As a result of this directive, member states are likely to be extending and improving their provisions, especially where existing provision excludes indirect discrimination.

The USA, Canada, Australia and South Africa all have specific legislation against direct and indirect racial discrimination, and all except Australia have a variety of requirements for affirmative action by employers. In the USA there is compulsory reporting of workforce monitoring to the specialised body, and government contractors are required to take affirmative action to reduce disparities. Canada too requires employers to report annually on the representation of designated groups, and federal contractors are required to take affirmative action. South Africa requires employers to analyse the composition of their workforce, have an employment equity plan and take affirmative action.

Many European countries have a form of specialist body for dealing with racial discrimination, but there is a wide variety in their functions and powers. Some, in France, Germany, Denmark and Portugal, are mainly advisory. Others, in Belgium, Sweden, Great Britain, Ireland, and the Netherlands, have legal powers. Most specialist bodies also cover all protected groups. Specialist bodies in Australia, the USA and Canada also have legal powers. In these countries, and in South Africa, government departments are also involved in monitoring and regulation of affirmative action requirements.

Legal measures against hate speech, activities, and hate crime

There is a wide variety of approaches to the defining and banning of racist material, behaviour and speech. Often the approach depends on the history and experience of the country concerned. For example, experience of the Nazis in the Second World War has led countries such as France, Italy, Austria and Germany to focus on banning certain extremist organisations, and holocaust denial. Other countries including Ireland, Sweden, Great Britain and the Netherlands have legislation against incitement to racial hatred. At the other extreme, the USA does not prohibit racist speech and material because of the conflict with the right to free speech, but some states have banned the burning of religious symbols and wearing certain masks.

Hate crimes, defined as racially motivated violence, are treated in one of three ways. They may be treated as a general criminal offence, or as a general offence with increased penalties for racial motivation. The third way is to have specific racially motivated offences. Several countries have a mixture of offences in all three categories. The advantage of treating racial violence as a general offence is that it is not necessary to prove a racial motivation for an attack, the evidence for which is difficult to obtain. However, having specific offences or enhanced penalties for racist motivation sends a clear signal that such crimes are particularly serious and unacceptable.

Because of the wide variations in the approach to racist speech, incidents and crime, it is impossible to compare statistics between different countries. Some countries such as Great Britain record reported racist offences according to the victims' perceptions. Other countries such as Germany define them according to definitions of the authorities, in which case there normally has to be some evidence of a racial motivation. Where the definition is subjective, official statistics on the incidence of racial harassment and violence are likely to be much higher than in countries where the authorities define the offence.

Promoting diversity

All the countries covered in this paper have programmes to promote tolerance and to discourage racial discrimination and racism. Many European governments publish information about the positive contribution of ethnic minorities. Examples include Germany which publishes a quarterly journal and regular statistical bulletins, Britain which publishes a wide range of statistical information on the position of ethnic minorities, and the Netherlands which publishes an annual Integration Monitor, and a variety of detailed statistical reports. Many governments are directly involved in promoting tolerance, and they also channel responsibility to the specialist bodies to organise information campaigns against racism and challenge negative stereotypes. Examples include the Centre for Equal Opportunities and Opposition to Racism in Belgium, the Commission for Racial Equality in Britain, and the Anti-discrimination Bureaux (LBR) in the Netherlands. In many instances there are local bodies too organising at the municipal and regional level. Britain, the Netherlands, Norway, Denmark and Sweden are among European countries with active programmes to improve the representation of ethnic minority people in national and local government services. Several governments have also issued codes of good practice to give practical advice on promoting equal opportunities.

In the USA, the main focus of the government is on technical advice and information on compliance with government contract requirements, and with the requirements of the Civil Rights Act, and government departments have affirmative action programmes. The Uniform Guidelines provide definitive joint advice from several departments on compliance with the law. Canada and South Africa also have employment equity and affirmative action programmes for government services. Canada and Australia have active inter-cultural programmes in relevant departments including education and programmes for promoting tolerance and the benefits of diversity.

Although it is generally accepted that ethnicity data is needed to evaluate levels of discrimination and to measure progress towards achieving racial equality, most European countries do not have such data. They use statistics on nationality and birthplace for national monitoring, but organisations do not generally monitor their activities. The Netherlands and Great Britain are the only countries in Europe to have data on the ethnic origin of the population. Both countries publish a range of indicators for use in local and workplace monitoring. The USA and Canada have very detailed census and other statistics on race and ethnicity. Australia uses census data on birthplace, religion, language and ancestry. South Africa collects data on population groups and the Statistics Council publishes a wide range of socio-economic material.

Conclusion

The USA, Canada, Australia, countries which were largely founded on immigration, and South Africa, have the most comprehensive civil legislation against discrimination, including requirements to take affirmative or positive action in defined circumstances. These countries also have good data for measuring and evaluating progress. The USA and South Africa in particular have concentrated more on compliance than on encouraging voluntary efforts and on promoting tolerance.

In contrast, the emphasis in many European countries had been on encouraging tolerance with the main focus of legislation on the prevention of hate speech and organisation of fascist and racist groups. Britain and the Netherlands have the most comprehensive anti-discrimination laws in Europe, including positive duties. These two countries also have reasonable data on ethnic background for monitoring progress. In future, the position in EU member states is likely to change as the racial discrimination directive is implemented.

Countries with comprehensive legal approaches and reasonable data such as the USA, Britain and the Netherlands can show some signs of improvement in the position of ethnic minorities. Comparisons with other countries are difficult because of incomplete data.

1. Introduction

This paper considers approaches to achieving racial equality in several member states of the European Union (EU), and also in other racially diverse countries with active policies and programmes. These include the United States, Canada, Australia and South Africa.

The information in this paper is from published sources, including that available from searches of official government and international web-sites. There has not been an opportunity to make any direct enquiries to bring published information up to date, and we welcome details of any recent developments in the countries mentioned.

The primary purpose of this paper is to provide a comparative overview of the different approaches in a consistent framework. There are different historical, legal, civil and economic circumstances in all the countries referred to which affect their approach, and these make comparisons problematic. For this reason we have not attempted to draw any conclusions about the effectiveness of different systems.

International standards, that is, those of The International Convention on the Elimination of All forms of Racial Discrimination (CERD) and the Council of Europe have been used as the basic yardsticks against which to compare what is being done.[2]

Scope

The paper looks at action by governments to achieve racial equality. It reviews:

- legal measures to combat racial discrimination;
- legal and other measures to combat hate crimes, racism and intolerance; and
- activities being taken by governments to promote the benefits of tolerance and diversity.

There are of course many invaluable activities being carried out by non-governmental organisations, especially those which campaign and act against racism and discrimination and offer support and assistance to victims of racism and discrimination. Many employers, too, have active equal opportunities and diversity programmes. It is beyond the scope of this paper to review action by NGOs and others outside government.

---

2. For the full text of all relevant international conventions, see Council of Europe Press: 'Human Rights in International Law'

Several of the countries featured have a federal government system and provinces or states are carrying out a significant range of activities in the areas covered. Again, it is not possible to include comprehensive information about action being taken by regional or local governments, although a few examples are included.

Terminology

Many different terms are used in different countries to describe people of immigrant origin. In most EU member states, the latter term is equivalent to 'people from the ethnic minorities' which is preferred in countries with a long history of immigration such as the UK and the Netherlands. In the USA, Australia and Canada, the terms 'minorities', 'ethnic minorities' or 'visible minorities' may be used. In South Africa, the black African population has historically suffered from state-sponsored discrimination and severe disadvantage, but this population is of course neither a minority nor of immigrant origin.

This paper is concerned primarily with the visible ethnic minorities who are particularly vulnerable to racism, racial discrimination and disadvantage. They may or may not be of immigrant origin.

2.   The context

Europe's ethnic minorities

There are some significant differences in the ways in which European states record their ethnic minority populations, which make comparisons difficult. In part these differences reflect differences in migration histories and policy approaches to migration. For example, in the 1960s and early 1970s, western and northern European countries such as Germany and Belgium attracted temporary migrant workers or 'guest-workers' first from southern Europe and later from northern Africa and Turkey, to meet demand for labour. Although most of these temporary migrants put down roots and stayed in their receiving countries, they retained their 'foreigner' status. Until recently the majority of these immigrants and their descendants were of foreign citizenship.

Other countries such as the Netherlands, France, the UK and more recently Portugal, attracted labour from their former colonies, and many of these were nationals of their receiving country. As international migration data is based on records of foreigners, these data provide only very rough estimates of the visible ethnic minority populations.

Care also has to be taken to distinguish between foreigners who are nationals of other EU member states. Another difficulty in comparing immigration data is that there is no international standardised reporting system. Some countries use population registers, others rely on residence or work permits (OECD, 1999).

By the mid-1970s the need for labour had reduced and most western European governments restricted immigration and limited it mainly to family reunion. Although immigration slowed, it nevertheless continued and with family reunion and the higher fertility of immigrants because of their younger age profile, visible populations of immigrant origin became established. There is now a second and third generation of visible ethnic minorities in many western European countries.

Since 1997, immigration into countries such as the UK, Sweden, the Netherlands, Germany and France has been linked to the growth in asylum seekers and of refugees from conflicts in the former Yugoslavia, Somalia and Iraq (OECD, 1999).

The best estimate of the overall immigrant population from outside the EU is about 4.5 per cent (Eurostat, 1995), of which the largest group originates from Turkey, followed by those who originate from the former Yugoslavia and from Morocco and Algeria. These statistics are, however, based on nationality, and exclude naturalised immigrants and the descendants of immigrants, or ethnic minorities. Thus the EU's ethnic minority population is much larger: about five per cent rising to a possible eight per cent depending on definitions.

Countries with the largest immigrant and ethnic minority populations are Austria, Belgium, France, Germany, the Netherlands and the United Kingdom.

It is estimated that about 20 per cent of the French-born population now has one parent or grandparent of immigrant origin (Tribalat, 1991).

Luxembourg has a large population of immigrants, mainly from other EU countries, especially Portugal and Italy.

Countries in central and eastern Europe do not have a significant visible minority population from immigration. The main ethnic minority groups in this area are Roma people, whose presence dates back over 400 years. Accurate statistics are not available but estimates indicate that the highest proportions are in Bulgaria, the Czech Republic, Romania and Slovakia, where the Roma are between nine and twelve per cent of the population (Council of Europe, 1998).

Racial discrimination and disadvantage

Europe

Whatever the origin of Europe's visible ethnic minority population, they tend to be disproportionately unemployed, and to suffer from racial discrimination and disadvantage. Research by the ILO in Belgium, Denmark, Finland, France, Germany, the Netherlands, Spain, Sweden and the UK shows that ethnic minority workers are disproportionately under-employed or unemployed and face discrimination (Zegers de Beijl [Undated] and ILO, 1998).

Using standardised methods with matched white and ethnic minority applicants, the ILO showed that discrimination against the ethnic minority applicant was widespread. Discrimination rates varied between 33 and 37 per cent. Similar tests conducted in the UK showed that one in three employers discriminated against the ethnic minority applicant (McIntosh et al., 1974).

Table 1: ***Labour force and unemployment rates of immigrants in selected European countries (1996)***

Country	Percentage of foreigners in labour force	Foreign unemployment rate		National unemployment rate	
		Female	Male	Female	Male
Belgium	8.1	31.5	19.8	11	6
Denmark	2.2		16.2	8.4	5.4
France	6.3	24.4	20.2	13.6	9.2
Germany	8.9	14.8	15.1	9.2	6.1
Netherlands	3.8	24.3	23.1	8.2	5.3
Norway	2.6				
Sweden	4.4	15.6	23.5	7	8.1
UK	3.5	11.7	16.4	6.7	9.8

Source: OECD. Data are from a variety of national sources, such as population registers or labour force surveys, and refer to foreign nationals only.

Outside Europe

Immigrants, at first mainly from Europe, largely populated the USA during the last 300 years. Today, minorities, defined as black and Hispanic Americans, are a growing proportion of the population. Black or African-American people are twelve per cent of the population and are growing in the labour market at almost twice the rate of the white population. People of Hispanic-origin are ten per cent of the population (Bendick et al, 1998) and are growing in the labour market five times faster than the non-Hispanic population (US Department of Labor, 1988). In addition, the USA continues to receive immigrants. About ten per cent of US residents were born outside the USA, the largest proportion being Hispanics (32 per cent) and Asians (25 per cent).

Canada is also a country of immigrants, initially from Europe (Britain and France), and still has one of the highest levels of immigration in the world. Canada currently has an immigrant population of just under 18 per cent. Many recent immigrants are skilled and more than one third has higher education qualifications. The proportion of immigrants from Asia is now 31 per cent with Hong Kong and China the largest groups (OECD, 1999). Others come from Latin and Central America and the Caribbean.

As in Europe, visible ethnic minorities in North America suffer disproportionately from racial disadvantage and discrimination. Situation tests carried out for the ILO using the standard methodology, referred to under 'Racial discrimination and disadvantage' above, showed that the rate of discrimination faced by black applicants was 19.4 per cent and that for Hispanic applicants was over 33 per cent (Bendick, 1996).

Since the 1970s, Canada also experienced incidents of intolerance and increased discrimination against visible ethnic minorities (Ventura,1995).

Like Canada, Australia is a country of immigration and 23 per cent of the current population was born overseas. Again, like Canada, immigrants, in the 60s and 70s were mainly from Europe, especially Britain and Ireland. Since the early 1980s, the majority of immigrants were from Asia, and by 1996 22 per cent of the overseas-born population came from Asia. Asians are now five per cent of the total population. There are also indigenous aboriginal people who are two per cent of the population. The aboriginal people suffer serious social and economic disadvantages, and there has been opposition from established second generation white people from Britain and other European countries to recent immigrants from Asia.

Unlike the other countries featured, South Africa's visible minority is white and economically dominant. Under apartheid, the black majority suffered from state-sanctioned discrimination and exclusion and the great majority are still disadvantaged. The white population is just under six per cent with Africans forming almost 77 per cent of the total, 'coloured' or mixed race people almost nine per cent, and Indian and other Asian origin people 2.6 per cent of the population (South African Statistics Council, Census 96, 1999)[3].

3.   Successful racial equality strategies

Experience in all ethnically diverse countries demonstrates that where ethnic minority people experience racial discrimination and disadvantage, the causes are accumulative and inter-related and can become entrenched and persistent across generations. Experience also indicates that a combination of measures is needed to achieve equality of opportunity and to remove deep-seated barriers to full participation in economic, social and public spheres (Coussey, 2000a; ILO., 2000; Council of Europe, 2000).

Although this paper concentrates on some fundamental measures by governments, such as implementing anti-discrimination legislation, taking effective action against racism and hate crimes and promoting equality, these are not the only steps needed. It is important to recognise that action is needed to remove barriers to participation by all organisations concerned with education, access to training and employment, housing, health, social welfare, participation in cultural, civic and public life.

The 1965 UN Convention on the Elimination of all Forms of Racial Discrimination (CERD) requires contracting states to take a wide range of action to ensure that there is no discrimination.

Some key provisions include:

- specific legislation against discrimination;
- legislation against the dissemination of ideas promoting racial superiority, hatred and violence;
- encouraging multi-racial organisations;
- guaranteeing equality before the law;
- countering prejudice and promoting tolerance in education, culture and the provision of information; and
- special measures (positive action) to enable minority groups to take advantage of opportunities.

---

4.   Legal measures to combat racial discrimination

According to established minimum international standards, national legislation protecting people from racial discrimination based on race, colour, descent, or national or ethnic origin should include the following:

---

1. Be unlawful in employment and the supply of goods, facilities and services *(i.e. in the political, economic, social, cultural or any other field of public life [CERD]).*

2. Appropriate redress and support for individual victims, and easy access to adjudication.

3. Provisions covering direct and indirect acts of discrimination *(i.e. any distinction, exclusion, restriction or preference [CERD]).*

4. Provision for positive or affirmative action *(i.e. special measures for the sole purpose of securing adequate advancement [CERD]).*

5. Independent specialist bodies to promote equality of opportunity and to monitor the implementation of anti-discrimination legislation.

(Zegers de Beijl [Undated]; ILO., 1998; Council of Europe, 1998 and 2000; and European Commission against Racism and Intolerance [ECRI], 1997).

Civil or criminal legislation?

Europe

European countries have met their international obligations to legislate against racial discrimination in two ways. Some have specifically enacted legislation against racial discrimination, and others rely on general constitutional provisions against racial discrimination. Another difference is whether breaches of the provisions are criminal or civil offences, and in several instances such as France and Denmark, there are both civil and criminal provisions against discrimination.

Countries with general constitutional provisions include Austria, France, Germany, Italy and Spain. Countries with specific provisions in the criminal code include Belgium, Denmark, France, Italy, Norway and Portugal (Council of Europe, ECRI, 1998a).

Countries with specific civil legal provisions against racial discrimination in employment, and the provision of facilities and services, include Denmark, Ireland, Netherlands, Norway, Sweden and the UK.

Finland, France, Germany and Spain have provisions in labour codes and workplace collective agreements relating mainly to discriminatory conditions (ILO, 1998).

Positive or affirmative action

Europe
At the moment, only Great Britain and the Netherlands have provision in the legislation for indirect discrimination and for affirmative or positive action. In both countries this is permissive, not obligatory.

In Great Britain, the Race Relations Act 1976 allows employers to encourage people from under-represented groups to apply for work in which they are under-represented, and to provide training to help them compete for work in which they are under-represented. The exception is in Northern Ireland where, under the Fair Employment and Treatment Order, employers are required to take affirmative action where monitoring and reviews show that there is a lack of fair participation of one community.

In the Netherlands, the Employment of Minorities (Promotion) Act allows employers to take measures to encourage the employment of ethnic minorities and to ensure that ethnic minority employees participate within the workforce (Fourteenth CERD report, 1999).

The EU Council Directive 2000 requires member states to enact provisions by 2003 to prevent direct and indirect racial discrimination in employment, occupation, access to training, social protection, education and the provision of goods, facilities and services.

The directive allows positive action to compensate for racially or ethnically-linked disadvantages and requires member states to have adequate support for victims and to designate a specialist body to promote equal treatment and monitor levels of discrimination.

As a result of this directive, member states are likely to be extending and improving their provisions, especially where existing provision excludes indirect discrimination.

Those countries with racial discrimination provisions in criminal codes - which have a higher burden of proof than in civil legislation – will need to legislate to ensure that enforcement of individual rights is easier. Countries with no independent or expert support will also have to make provision for this.

Outside Europe

Australia, Canada, South Africa and the USA all have specific legislation preventing racial discrimination in employment and services.

Canada has a federal Human Rights Act 1985 and similar laws at provincial level. It also has an Employment Equity Act 1988 (affirmative action), which covers employers within federal jurisdiction. Ontario has provincial employment equity legislation covering all employers (Ventura, 1995).

Australia has a Racial Discrimination Act 1975 covering direct and indirect discrimination in employment, and also state anti-discrimination legislation.

The USA also has both federal and state legislation. Title VII of the 1964 Civil Rights Act outlaws direct discrimination in employment, and practices with disparate impact (indirect discrimination). It also has the 1965 Executive Order 11246, which establishes the federal contract compliance programme under which contractors must take affirmative action to redress under-utilisation of minorities, and other groups. Discrimination in other areas such as accommodation and education is covered in a variety of federal and state laws, mostly requiring private civil action in courts.

South Africa has an Employment Equity Act which outlaws direct and indirect discrimination and requires affirmative action to reduce under-representation, and a Promotion of Equality and Prevention of Unfair Discrimination Act which covers non-employment.

Positive duties and compulsory monitoring

Studies have recognised a further regulatory stage in which governments and employers are required to take action to overcome structural discrimination and to achieve fair participation in access to work. In most instances positive requirements apply to employment only, but there are a few examples of positive duties applied to public services (Department of Justice, 1996; ILO., 1998; Hepple, 2000).

The argument for this approach is that it requires employers actively to tackle all the causes of under-representation of particular ethnic minorities. This has been shown to be more effective for achieving equality of opportunity than reliance on individual complaints and voluntary codes of practice and monitoring. Legally required positive duties and monitoring are found in the Netherlands, Great Britain, Northern Ireland, the USA, Canada and South Africa.

Employers in the Netherlands also have to monitor the proportion of ethnic minorities in the workforce and implement plans to promote proportional representation.

Great Britain is currently consulting on the details of implementing a similar scheme for promoting racial equality in public services.

In Northern Ireland employers have to monitor the religious composition of the workforce, and report this annually to the Equality Commission, periodically review their practices and take affirmative action to reduce any under-representation of one community. There are also requirements for public authorities to review and monitor their functions and access to their services, to assess the impact on equality of opportunity.

In the USA, workforce monitoring and reporting to the specialised body, the Equal Employment Opportunities Commission, is compulsory, and an executive order (11246) requires employers to take affirmative action to reduce under-representation as a condition of being an approved government contractor.

In Canada, employers have to report annually on the representation of designated groups in the workforce and adopt positive measures if they are government contractors.

In South Africa, the Department of Labour enforces the Employment Equity Act through labour inspectors who may issue compliance orders. Employers are required to register with an employment equity register, to analyse their practices and the composition of the workforce, have an employment equity plan, including numerical goals, and take affirmative action to achieve a representative workforce. State contractors have to obtain a certificate of compliance from the Minister of Labour.

Specialist bodies

Countries with some form of specialised body for dealing with racial discrimination include Australia, Belgium, Canada, Denmark, France, Germany, Ireland, Netherlands, Norway, South Africa, Sweden, UK and the USA.

However, these have a wide variety of functions and powers. Some are mainly concerned with monitoring the legislation and advising government.

> **Specialist bodies, mainly advisory and monitoring**
>
> - Denmark: Board for Ethnic Equality
> - France: Discrimination Research Group and designated commissions under the Prefecture in each département for access to citizenship (CODAC)
> - Germany: Commission for Foreigners
> - Portugal: High Commissioner for immigration and Ethnic Minorities

Others have powers to bring cases.

> **Specialist bodies with legal powers**
>
> - Australia: Human Rights and Equal Opportunities Commission
> - Belgium: Centre for Equality of Opportunity and Opposition to Racism
> - Canada: Human Rights Commission
> - Ireland: Equality Authority
> - Netherlands: Equal Treatment Commission
> - Norway: Centre for Combating Ethnic Discrimination
> - Sweden: Ombudsman against Ethnic Discrimination
> - UK: Commission for Racial Equality and Equality Commission for Northern Ireland
> - USA: the Equal Employment Opportunities Commission, and the Office for Civil Rights (for education.)

Only Belgium, Denmark, Great Britain and Norway have separate specialised bodies for race equality. The others are responsible for all protected categories.

In Canada, Northern Ireland, South Africa, and the USA, where legislation covers employment equity and positive duties, these bodies also have wider monitoring and regulatory powers. However, in the USA enforcement is also by the Office of Federal Contract Compliance, which is now the Employment Standards Administration (Details in Table 2). Australia, Canada and the USA also have state or province-level enforcement agencies.

Making the anti-discrimination legislation effective

Several international bodies such as the ILO have commented on the need for the allocation of adequate support and resources to promote compliance with the law. It is an explicit requirement of Article 2 of CERD that contracting states take 'all appropriate means' to eliminate discrimination. As a minimum, there has to be the provision of information about rights, advice and assistance to the victims of discrimination, and measures to inform the public about the requirements of the legislation. In countries with a specialised body for dealing with discrimination, these bodies play a central role in promoting awareness of the law. For example, in Sweden the Ombudsman against Ethnic Discrimination publishes brochures, arranges conferences, and awareness campaigns.

In Britain, the Commission for Racial Equality publishes practical guidance on how to comply with the law, and the government and social partners have also published practical guidance.

The EEOC in the USA publishes guidance and the Department of Labor also provides technical advice on compliance with the contracting requirements. The EEOC, Department of Labor, Justice and the Civil Service Commission have produced definitive rules on employee selection procedures (Federal Register Title 29, 1978).

Similarly, this is an important role for the Canadian Human Rights Commission and the Australian Human Rights and Equal Opportunities Commission. Government-backed codes of practice can also help raise awareness of the legal requirements (see Chapter 6, Promoting good practice). It is more difficult to provide this focus where there is no specialised anti-discrimination body.

A different approach has been taken in France where action for reviewing cases lies with the 115 CODACs. The government has distributed brochures, and set up a free telephone number – 114 – which victims can use to obtain information on their rights and obtain support.

Table 2   *Comparison of anti-discrimination legislation in selected countries*

	Main legislation	Outlawed grounds	Scope	Specialised body	Monitoring and positive duties
Australia	Civil: Racial Discrimination Act 1975	Race, colour, descent, ethnic or national origin	Employment, goods & services	Race Discrimination Commissioner (Human Rights Commission)	No
Belgium	Criminal Code 1994	Race, colour, nationality, ethnic or national origin	Employment, goods & services	Centre pour l'Egalite des Chances et la Lutte Contre le Racisme	No
Canada	Civil: Human Rights Act 1985	Includes religion, sex, marital and family status, disability and pardoned convicted	Employment, goods & services	Human Rights Commission	Yes, for federal contractors
Denmark	Criminal: Prohibition of racial discrimination 1971 (services) Civil: Prohibition of Discrimination in Labour Market 1996	Includes religion & political conviction	Employment, goods & services	Board for Ethnic Equality (Advisory)	No
France	Criminal code: Services & offers of employment 1994 Labour code	Origin, race or religion	Recruitment dismissal, goods & services	Commissions departmentales d'access a la Citoyennete (advisory)	No
Germany	Civil: Works Council Constitution Act, Federal Civil Servants Act	Parentage, sex, religion, origin, political or union activities	Treatment at work. Recruitment to civil service.	Commissioner for Foreigners (Advisory)	No

	Main legislation	Outlawed grounds	Scope	Specialised body	Monitoring and positive duties
Netherlands	Civil: Equal Treatment Act 1994 Employment of Minorities (Promotio) Act 1998	Religion, belief, political opinion, race, sex, sexual orientation, or civil status	Employment, goods & services	Equal Treatment Commission	Yes
South Africa	Employment Equity Act 1998 Promotion of Equality/ Prevention of Unfair Discrimination Act 2000	Race, colour, ethnic or social origin, sex, sexual orientation, age, disability, conscience belief, culture or language	Employment, goods & services	None	Yes
Sweden	Civil: Act against Ethnic Discrimination 1994, Act against Discrimination in Working Life 1999. Criminal code-services	Race, colour, national or ethnic origin, or religious creed	Employment & services	Ombudsman against Ethnic Discrimination	No
UK	Civil: Race Relations Acts 1976/2000 Fair employment and Treatment Order (NI)	Race colour, ethnic or national origin, or nationality (GB) Religious belief and political opinion (NI)	Employment, goods & services	Commission for Racial Equality Equality Commission (NI)	Yes, public bodies and in Northern Ireland
USA	Civil: Civil Rights Act 1964/91 Executive Order 11246	Race, colour, religion, national origin or sex	Employment, goods & services	Equal Employment Opportunity Commission Office for Civil Rights	Yes

5. Legal measures to combat hate speech and hate crimes

Definition

Article 4 of the Convention on the Elimination of all Forms of Racial Discrimination (CERD) defines hate activities as:

All those which are based on ideas or theories of superiority of one race or group of one colour or ethnic origin, which justify or promote racial hatred or discrimination.

CERD requires signatories to make it an offence to disseminate such ideas, and to incite discrimination or violence. It also requires signatories to prohibit organisations and organised activities to incite racial hatred and discrimination.

Why action is needed to combat hate activities

The dissemination of racist ideas, racist activities, and racial harassment and violence are a threat to the cohesion and stability of multi-racial and pluralist societies. These activities are profoundly disturbing and frightening to people from the ethnic minorities and create a sense of insecurity and helplessness. In many countries where there are visible ethnic minorities and also where there is continuing immigration, it is common for immigrants and ethnic minorities to be portrayed negatively and in emotional terms. They are seen as a cause of social problems, worsening unemployment, crime and cultural conflicts.

Negative portrayal of visible minorities and immigrants encourages social distance and hostility, and this in turn encourages discrimination. Racist violence is the extreme expression of negative and hostile views and may be partly encouraged or legitimised by a climate in which the dissemination of racially derogatory materials or words is allowed. For these reasons many countries try to control the dissemination of such material.

Racial violence has been linked in public discussion to the size and concentration of the visible ethnic minority population, or to recent migration, but this does not explain the presence of such violence in areas such as eastern Germany where there is a very small minority population. Racial violence has also been linked to economic uncertainty and unemployment, but it is not predominantly carried out by disadvantaged or unemployed people. Most such explanations are too simplistic. However, the general social and political climate has been shown to be important, and so too has the way that authorities respond, especially the police (Bjorgo and Witte, 1993).

This is supported by the Eurobarometer survey for the European Monitoring Centre. The survey concluded that party political affiliation is part of the causal system producing attitudes towards minorities. Political leadership is very significant for the quarter of the EU population who are ambivalent towards ethnic minorities because they are the ones who react most to political leadership (Talhammer et al., 2001).

Experience demonstrates that a proactive strategy is necessary to try and prevent the dissemination of racist material. Legislation is only one element of a strategy. Action is needed to create a positive public climate, including promoting tolerance and diversity, public education of the benefits of diversity and of immigration. Activities to promote tolerance and the benefits of diversity are dealt with in the next section. This section looks at the legislation against intolerant behaviour.

Defining racist violence, hate activities and crime

There is no comparative data on the incidence of intolerant behaviour because of the very wide variety of approaches to defining and recording such incidents. The main difficulty is in determining whether to tackle racist behaviour under existing criminal and civil legislation, or whether to enact specific legislation (Cowl, 1995).

The following questions are relevant:

- What type of acts should be banned? Racially derogatory or offensive material? Or only material which incites violence or discrimination?
- What is the balance between freedom of expression and preventing racially offensive material?
- Should racist organisations be banned or only activities that incite racial hatred?
- What is the balance between freedom of association and the prevention of racist organisations?
- Which activities should be criminal and which are civil offences?
- How can racial motivation or hate be proved? If racially motivated offences are under a separate hate crimes statute rather than criminal law, it is necessary to prove racial motivation, which is more difficult than under normal criminal statutes.

There are, not surprisingly, different approaches to these questions, depending on the particular recent history, experience and concerns of the country concerned. Some countries record offences motivated by racial violence, others concentrate on monitoring the activities of far-right or racist groups. There are also wide differences in the initial definitions of racially motivated offences and incidents. They may be defined subjectively, according to the perspective of the victim, or according to the ethnic origin of perpetrators and victims, or according to the definition of the police or prosecuting authority. Police and prosecuting authorities may require some overt expression of racial motivation.

There may be generic offences of disseminating racist propaganda, racial harassment or violence, or specified offences such as holocaust denial. Some countries allow unrestricted freedom of expression or freedom of association, and racist activity only becomes an offence when linked to violence or threatened violence.

There is also the problem of 'low level' or everyday racism, such as name-calling, displays of antagonism and social avoidance and segregation. There is a continuum of distancing behaviour which, if discouraged, can lead to more overt and threatening actions. Discouraging low level racism is an important preventive measure and is dealt with under the next heading.

Attempts by the EU to monitor racism and xenophobia found it impossible to make any comparisons because of the differences in classifications of offences, differences in data collection, and the differences in legislation. (European Monitoring Centre on Racism and Xenophobia, EUMC, 1998). EUMC can only list the incidence of different offences as reported by each member state, and they are clearly not comparable.

Preventing the dissemination of hate speech, displays and publications

Europe
Until recently, certain western European countries have put greater emphasis on specific regulations against hate speech and racist organisations than they have on legislating against racial discrimination. These countries tend to be influenced by their experience of the Nazis in the Second World War. For example, in France the government can ban by decree particular organisations involved in inciting racial discrimination, hatred or violence, or which vindicate war crimes. The penal code makes it an offence to wear or display Nazi badges or emblems and to wear uniforms associated with organisations involved with crimes against humanity. Contesting crimes against humanity, particularly the holocaust, is also an offence (Council of Europe, 1998).

Similarly, the German penal code makes it an offence to incite hatred or violence against certain groups, disseminate racial hatred and deny the holocaust. Certain extremist organisations have been banned.

Italy has similar provisions in its criminal code, and bans the formation of the fascist party, and Austria also bans racially motivated insults as well as the National Socialist Party.

Spain bans incitement to racial hatred and holocaust denial (European Monitoring Centre on Racism and Xenophobia, EUMC, 1998).

Most other western European countries have created general criminal offences against incitement to racial hatred. For example, this is the approach in Great Britain, Ireland, the Netherlands and Sweden. England and Wales prohibits the chanting of racist slogans at football matches. Several western countries including Denmark, Great Britain, the Netherlands, Norway and Sweden do not ban extremist groups, but rely on legislation to control their activities.

Several countries have recently been concerned about the possibilities of limiting racist communications on the Internet. As with preventing racist speech and materials, there are many different approaches. Some countries define the Internet as telecommunications, others as publishing, others as broadcasting. Germany has new legislation to deal with the Internet, and others such as the UK have updated existing legislation to include electronic transmissions (De Santis, 1998).

The Netherlands has a Reporting Centre for Discrimination on the Internet (MDI) which warns and asks for the removal of offending material and, if this fails, reports the matter to the police[4].

Outside Europe

The United States is restrained from taking action against hate speech and material by potential conflicts with the First Amendment in the Constitution which protects the right to free speech. Exceptions to this include threatening words which direct action towards breaches of the peace and violence. Although many states have enacted laws against racist or hate crimes, some of these have been ruled to be in conflict with the right to free speech. In other instances specific prosecutions have been overturned on these grounds (Cowl, 1995). There are also provisions against burning religious symbols (crosses) and wearing masks and hoods except for theatrical and carnival dress.

---

4.   Report submitted by the Netherlands to the UN Committee on the Elimination of racial Discrimination, 1999

Canada's federal criminal code covers the dissemination of hate propaganda, incitement of hatred and wilful promotion of hatred (Department of Justice, 1995). It is expected to be effective against Internet communications.

There is no federal legislation against hate speech, although this is currently the subject of public debate. Several states have enacted legislation against vilification on racial grounds. The Race Relations Act includes civil prohibition of insulting, humiliating or intimidating behaviour on racial grounds (De Santis, 1998).

South Africa's constitution includes a right to human dignity, and an independent Human Rights Commission promotes observance of the constitution. The Commission promotes diversity and tolerance through publications and conferences, for example it is running a 'Roll Back Xenophobia' campaign. The Commission has recently considered allegations of racism in the press, and made a series of detailed proposals for sensitising the media and to encourage the understanding of inclusivity and cultural diversity. A debate is currently in progress on the balance between freedom of expression and speech enshrined in the constitution, and the need to prevent racist material and speech.

Racial violence

As indicated under the section on 'Why action is needed to combat hate activities', there are three approaches to dealing with racist violence:

- treat it as a general criminal offence;
- have increased penalties for offences in which a racial motivation is established; and
- have specific racially-motivated offences.

The advantage of treating racial violence as a general offence is that there is no need to prove that the action was racially motivated. Such evidence is often difficult to obtain, and may make a successful prosecution more difficult. The advantage of having specific offences or increased penalties for racial motivation is that it makes it clear that the authorities regard them as particularly serious and unacceptable.

Germany, Norway, Spain, and Sweden do not have specific offences, but have increased penalties for offences in which racial motivation is an aggravating factor. Austria has promotion of National Socialist aims as an aggravating factor in the criminal code (Council of Europe, 1998).

Great Britain has some specific racially aggravated offences and provisions for evidence of racial motivation to be considered as an aggravating factor in other offences. Belgium too has specific offences of incitement to racial hatred or violence. Some states in the USA have enhanced penalties for hate crimes. However, some countries such as Australia, Canada, France and Denmark have no legislative basis for putting forward a racist motivation for violent offences.

Recording and monitoring racially motivated incidents

Europe

There is no internationally comparable system for comparing racially motivated incidents. The Council of Europe has recommended that there should be a working definition based on the perception of the victim or any other incident, even if at the initial stage there is no objective evidence to establish a racial motivation (Oakley, 1997).

England and Wales have recently adopted this kind of definition as the basis for the collection of information on racist incidents (Home Office, 2000a). England and Wales also include a boosted ethnic minority sample in the annual Crime Survey which shows that ethnic minorities are more likely to be victims of household and personal offences than white people. It also provides information about ethnic minority victims' perceptions on whether the offence was racially motivated (Clancy et al, 2001).

In Germany the Federal Criminal Police Agency and state police agencies record offences motivated by xenophobia, defined as acts committed against individuals because of their ethnic origin, colour or appearance. The data collected and information on offenders is used as the basis for research into the genesis and patterns of racist behaviour. Co-ordination of detailed information about the incidence and nature of racist offences has been used to monitor and prevent the development of organised violent racist activities.

In the Netherlands, Anti-Discrimination Bureaux in over 40 cities collect information on reports of racial harassment and violence and incidents involving extremist activities. These are reported to the police. Regular liaison with the police can enable them to take preventive steps (Oakley, 1997). Norway's Centre for Combating Ethnic Discrimination monitors racially motivated crimes and the outcomes. Several countries including Austria, France and Germany, also monitor the activities of extremist groups (Oakley, 1996).

As with all monitoring by race and ethnic origin, keeping statistics is essential for reviewing the effectiveness of action, but it can also reveal uncomfortable facts about the extent of hate crimes. Because of the sensitivity of this data, some countries, for example, the Netherlands, do not publish it. There can also be considerable differences between the number of racist incidents reported to the authorities and those perceived to be racist by the victims. (For example, see the 1996 British Crime Survey.) However, as reports by the Council of Europe show, many member states do not have adequate systems for recording and monitoring hate crimes.[5]

Outside Europe

In the United States, monitoring is required under the federal Hate Crimes Statistics Act. The data from states and law enforcement agencies is collated and published annually by the Federal Bureau of Investigation – although there is known to be substantial under-recording.

Unlike the European examples given, there is no monitoring of hate groups themselves, as this would be perceived as an interference in the right of assembly (Cowl, 1995). Australia does not yet have a regular monitoring system for hate crimes, and considered that it had not reached crisis proportions (Council of Europe, ECRI, 1998a).

Although South Africa's recent main concern has been preventing politically motivated violence, there has been a history of state-sponsored racial violence under the apartheid system. The attitudes and behaviour associated with the former regime linger in the police and security forces. The government has been considering the possibility of legislating to make incitement to racial hatred a criminal offence by replacing old apartheid laws.

---

5.   For example, see the European Commission against Racism and Intolerance [ECRI] reports on Austria, Belgium, France.

Table 3   **Legal frameworks for banning racist material and racial violence in selected countries**

	Speech/ material/ symbols	Organised groups	Incitement to hatred/ violence	Specific offences of racial violence
Australia	no[6]	no	yes	no
Canada	yes	no	yes	no
Denmark	no	no	yes	no
France	yes	yes	yes	no
Germany	yes	yes	yes	yes
Netherlands	yes	no	yes	no
South Africa	no	no	no[7]	no
Sweden	no	no	yes	yes
UK	no	no	yes[8]	yes
USA	yes in some states	no	yes	yes in some states

6.   The Race Relations Act prohibits insulting racist behaviour
7.   Currently under consideration by the government
8.   Covers threatening violence not hatred

6.   Promoting diversity

What governments should do

Governments' main responsibility is to ensure that there is an effective legal and administrative structure for tackling racism, racial violence and discrimination. But governments have a significant leadership function. They should:

- ensure that their own functions and employment practices are free of discrimination and are ethnically diverse;
- ensure that there is a positive approach to encouraging diversity and to meeting the needs of a diverse population;
- stimulate and encourage other national organisations to take action to prevent racial discrimination and promote diversity;
- make a difference to the climate of public debate, by encouraging tolerance and by condemning racism and xenophobia;
- make eliminating discrimination and promoting equal opportunities a priority in the allocation of funds and public grants;
- facilitate and stimulate action by other organisations, for example by providing start-up funding, contributing to joint funding and working in partnership with others; and
- disseminate facts and information about good practice and positive outcomes of integration projects (Coussey, 2000a).

Encouraging a positive public climate

Europe

There are many ways of creating a public climate which is open and inclusive. It is important for those in public life, especially national and local government representatives, to condemn racist and xenophobic speeches by politicians and others. It is necessary to disseminate information about the extent of racial discrimination and its effects, to help engage public support for positive measures against it. It is also important to disseminate positive information on the benefits of ethnic diversity, particularly on the economic and social contribution of ethnic minorities. There needs to be emphasis on joint participation and inclusion, and civic images, symbols and emblems should reflect this approach.

Many western European governments have initiated, supported and participated in campaigns against racism and racial discrimination. The most common way is for governments to channel responsibility for fighting racism and discrimination and to promote diversity to the specialist body (see Chapter 4, Positive duties and compulsory monitoring).

For example, the Belgian Centre for Equal Opportunities and Opposition to Racism organises campaigns to highlight the extent of discrimination in recruitment to raise public awareness of the problem, and to remind the public sector of its responsibilities (Centre for Equal Opportunities and Opposition to Racism, 2000).[9]

In Britain, the Commission for Racial Equality has a specific duty to promote equal opportunities and has run campaigns to raise public awareness of the nature and extent of discrimination, and to counter prejudice. Recent campaigns include posters to challenge negative stereotypes, campaigns to promote equality in sport, and a 'visible women' project to raise awareness of the problems facing ethnic minority women (Home Office, 15th Report to CERD).

Similarly, in the Netherlands, one of the main tasks of the local anti-discrimination bureaux, (LBR), partly funded by local municipalities, assisted by the national government, is to provide information about the nature and extent of racial discrimination.

The Office of the Ombudsman against Ethnic Discrimination in Sweden has worked particularly in schools to counter racism and prejudice, for example a film package was produced and offered to all secondary schools.

Several western European governments have also been directly involved in campaigns to promote tolerance and the benefits of diversity. For example, in Germany the federal government has been directly involved in such campaigns for a decade, and the president was involved in launching a programme to prevent violence and hostility against foreigners in 1992. This has continued and has been extended with the addition of a 'Network against Racism, for Equal Rights' which comprises 90 NGOs, with a detailed plan of action. The programme also includes federal and state sponsorship of a national 'Fairness and Understanding' campaign of posters and advertisements, aimed especially at young people, and measures to prevent violence and hostility at football matches. Fact sheets are prepared regularly to disseminate information on the economic contribution of minorities, including a quarterly journal 'Foreigners in Germany' ('AiD') to provide information about the positive contribution made by minorities. There is also a regular statistical bulletin on 'Foreigners in Germany' (Federal Ministry of Labour and Social Affairs, Statement 1996 in Council of Europe, ECRI, 1998b).

9.   see www.antiracisme.be/en/ceoor

In the Netherlands, several ministries have been directly involved in public education campaigns that stress the benefits of diversity. These included 'Young people against Intolerance' and 'Democracy means equality'. Both campaigns involved distributing pamphlets and advertising on television and video (Council of Europe, 2000b).

There has been research demonstrating the economic contribution of ethnic minorities to the Dutch labour market. (Bureau voor Economische Argumetatie, 1994). The government publishes an annual 'Integration Monitor' of key socio-economic indices of the extent of the ethnic minority population (Martens et al, 2000).

Great Britain has also published a wide range of statistical information on the position of ethnic minorities. These include an annual report on progress in the public services (Home Office, 2001a), and a study of the economic and social outcomes of migration. (Glover et al., 2001). The findings of research such as: the attitudes to crime of people from the ethnic minorities and also of the perpetrators of racial violence, and of the monitoring of the criminal justice system are also published (Mattison et al., 2000; Sibbitt, 1997; Home Office, 2000a).

Norway has carried out several awareness campaigns, aimed mainly at schools and young people (Council of Europe, ECRI, 1998b). Sweden has also allocated resources to a range of state agencies to develop measures against racism, focusing particularly on young people (Cowl, 1995).

It is also important to note that there are many activities at local level being supported and assisted by municipalities, and national governments. For example, Norway implemented a government–sponsored local Brumunddal Action Plan which became a model for co-operation between various government sectors in municipalities. France, Germany, Great Britain and Sweden also have local projects involving municipalities, and in France, departments, to raise awareness and take practical action to reduce racism (Council of Europe, 1995). In France, there is an official scheme which recognises the special role of women as mediators, 'Femmes Relais' (Bertaux et al, 1996).

Outside Europe

The system in the USA has relied mainly on the civil rights legislation, with individuals assisted by the EEOC. Administrative remedies, voluntary affirmative action and contract compliance all support this. Public attention to equality is maintained by the publicity given to court proceedings, and the high awards given. At state and city levels there are numerous programmes to promote diversity and tolerance, often channelled through community advocacy groups and supported by major corporations as part of their commitment to diversity.

Canada has had an active multi-cultural policy since the 1970s, which applies to all areas of cultural and social participation. A federal department of Multiculturalism and Citizenship has broad responsibilities to initiate and promote policies and programmes with respect to multiculturalism and citizenship, and to promote awareness of and participation in, Canada's multicultural heritage by all Canadians. Programmes include:

- the Race Relations and Cross-cultural Understanding programme to eliminate discrimination and ensure equal opportunities; and
- a Multi-Culturalism Secretariat to promote a co-ordinated approach among ministries (Cowl, 1995).

Most provinces in Canada also have programmes for promoting multi-culturalism and equity.

Australia, like Canada, has a multi-cultural policy and an Office of Multi-Cultural Affairs to encourage tolerance, and promote the benefits of diversity. There is a national strategy comprising Access and Equity, under which all government departments produce a three-year plan showing the obstacles to access and how these were being overcome (Cowl,1995).

South Africa has mainly concentrated on building a non-racial democracy and promoting inclusion and diversity has been a significant component. A massive national effort has been undertaken in all aspects of policy and its implementation to reconstruct an inclusive South African society. All ministries have been involved in this reconstruction.

Promoting diversity in government functions

For the sake of credibility, governments have to be seen to be in the lead in promoting diversity in their employment and in carrying out their functions. There are three strong efficiency arguments for governments to recruit representative proportions of ethnic minority people into the civil and public services.

1. labour markets in all developed economies are becoming increasingly competitive because of the ageing population and reduced number of new entrants to the labour market;

2. it is recognised that the provision of services and facilities to an ethnically diverse population is likely to be more sensitive to the needs of different communities if public service officials reflect that diversity; and

3. it is an important principle of representatives of democracy that the public services should be equally accessible to all taxpayers, both in national and local or regional government (Council of Europe, 1999).

Employment in the public services is normally open only to nationals of the country, but there is wide variation in what is defined as the public services. There are also significant differences in the nationality rules for public service employment. Some countries, for example, France, Portugal, the Netherlands and the UK, include certain categories of citizens of former colonial countries as nationals, and others accept third country nationals with settled status.

Until recently Germany had a low naturalisation rate of immigrants (Guild, 1999) and their descendants, because of more restrictive policies, making it difficult for active recruitment to the public services.

Germany and France also have widely defined rules limiting employment in the public services. For example, in France, foreigners are not permitted to work in the public utilities such as the railways, gas and electricity, licensed premises or tobacconists, casinos, nor as doctors and lawyers (Brouillet et al., 1999). In some countries some social security benefits are limited to nationals. The Council of Europe has drawn attention to the need for easier access to citizenship for settled immigrants (Council of Europe, 2000a).

Several European governments have made employment diversity in the public services a key part of their racial equality strategy. In two countries with the most comprehensive programmes, the UK and the Netherlands, these have a statutory basis, but the measures are voluntary in the remaining countries.

The UK civil service has had an active equal opportunities policy for over 20 years. It has collected data on the representation of ethnic minorities in different levels since 1989, and for several years has had a programme of action to focus on improving the recruitment, development and training of staff from the ethnic minorities, and training staff generally in equality practices. In 1999, the government set racial equality targets to measure performance in the provision of public services particularly in education, health, law and order, housing and local government (Home Office, 2000b and 2001a). Civil service departments also set racial equality targets for representation in the senior grades. Many local authorities have well-established racial equality programmes for employment and service provision. They are required to report their progress annually to the Audit Commission on a range of key performance indicators such as police recruitment. In 2000, legislation was enacted making it a statutory duty for certain public authorities to promote racial equality in carrying out their functions. This will require public authorities to be proactive (Home Office, 2001b).

The Netherlands has had an active programme for diversity in the public services since 1983. There have been two plans with targets for the employment of ethnic minorities in departments (EOM1 and EOM2) covering the period up to 1997, by which year there was 6.3 per cent representation (Council of Europe, 2000a). This has been succeeded by the Fair Employment of Ethnic Minorities Act, under which the government, with other employers, has to aim for proportional levels of employment for ethnic minorities and promote access at a wide range of levels.

Norway has a new plan of action for promoting the employment of ethnic minorities in central and local government and in state enterprises. This plan follows several earlier initiatives to encourage local authorities to devise local action plans, co-ordinated by the association of authorities. The Norwegian Directorate of Immigration and Department of Integration has taken a lead and has a target that ten per cent of its staff should be of an immigrant background.

Sweden began a series of new initiatives for improving diversity in state administration in 1997. Central government organised conferences and seminars to influence employment policy in government agencies, and the minister responsible for integration followed up with letters to all ministers and with enquiries on progress. Some agencies began a network to benchmark revised recruitment practice. The government provides financial support for a project, 'Sweden 2000', which campaigned to increase diversity in employment. The success of the various initiatives is being evaluated by the Agency for Administrative Development. Large city authorities, including the City of Stockholm, are also taking action such as encouraging ethnic minorities to apply for work in the authority.

Denmark has taken a series of initiatives at municipal and central government levels to improve the recruitment in the state sector. These include agreements with the Danish Central Federation of State Employees' organisations to set up local co-operation committees to implement the ethnic equality policy, and financial incentives to managers who recruited ethnic minorities and shared best practice .

Most governments in countries with long established ethnic minority populations have recognised the need for public officials to be trained in the principles and practice of equal opportunities. There are many different approaches to this, ranging from providing information on the law and on the cultural characteristics of ethnic minorities, changing behaviour by focusing on good practices, and challenging attitudes by raising awareness of unconscious prejudices and assumptions (Wrench et al., 1993). Priority is often given to officials who deal with the public especially those in employment and social services. Examples include the UK, Belgian and Norwegian employment services (Council of Europe, 2000b).[10]

Many countries have also given priority to police training, both training in combating racial discrimination and in intercultural communications. Police training schools in Denmark, Finland, France, Berlin, the Netherlands, Sweden and the UK all have comprehensive programmes for both new recruits and senior officers (Council of Europe, 1994).

Britain and the Netherlands have comprehensive training for many state officials, including those concerned with the administration of justice. Belgium began a programme of racial awareness training for judges in 1999.

Promoting good practice

There are three significant ways in which governments can influence the practices of other national organisations.

1.   They can provide resources for the specialist body for racial equality to promote good practice. In most cases these particularly concentrate on employment. For example, this is a primary function of the specialist bodies in Belgium, Denmark and the UK, and the racial discrimination bureaux of the Netherlands (see Chapter 4, Positive duties and compulsory monitoring).

---

10.   Report by Denmark to the UN Committee on the Elimination of Racial Discrimination, 2000

2. A second way for governments to influence practices is through the issue of codes. Again, most of these tend to be in employment although, in the UK, there is power to issue codes in employment, housing and social services. The employment code in the UK is semi-statutory in that its provisions can be taken into account in legal proceedings. There are voluntary employment codes in many Western European countries, including Belgium and the Netherlands. In Denmark, France and Germany, there are equality clauses in collective agreements which have a similar effect to codes of practice. Many of these codes and charters of good practice are produced at local level. One example is the Rotterdam Charter, an agreement between RADAR (the Rotterdam Anti-Discrimination Council), the Rotterdam Police and the Rotterdam municipality. There is also an international foundation with members from different European countries to promote good policing in multi-racial societies, and the Charter has been translated into eight other languages (Council of Europe, 2000a).

    There are also many other codes drawn up by private sector organisations such as employers' organisations, trade unions and the professions but these are outside the scope of this paper.

3. A third way for governments to influence is through their own advisory functions. Many state employment services pursue active labour market policies which include promoting diversity in employment. Several employment services have issued detailed guidance for staff on how to deal with discriminatory instructions, and these included a follow-up meeting with an employer at which advice on the legal requirements would be given. The UK also calls on the specialised Race Relations Advisory Services. Similarly, the Danish consultants for ethnic affairs carry out work in enterprises on employers' attitudes, and local German employment offices offer advice and assistance on diversity (Coussey, 2000b). There are also government-funded specialists to provide diversity awareness training. Examples include France, where the l'agence pour le développement des relations interculturelle (ADRI)[11] provides training for the public services and others concerned with integration on a range of subjects such as improving services to a multi-racial population and promoting equal opportunities. France also has the ASPECT Project, supported by the social partners and local public administration and employment services, which carries out training in the workplace (Council of Europe, 2000a).

There are many examples of government-funded training to enhance basic skills, improve job search and upgrade skills for entry into the labour market which particularly benefit people

---

11. see www.adri.fr/formation2001/pre.html

from disadvantaged ethnic minority groups. (Coussey, 2000b and Council of Europe, 2000b). There are also training schemes – positive action schemes – which are designed specifically for people from the ethnic minorities. These are not covered in this paper as the focus is on the positive promotion of diversity, rather than on reducing disadvantage.

Outside Europe

In the USA, government action has to be seen in the legal context, which has a compliance-based approach to equality and diversity. A major focus for fostering equal opportunities in the workplace is through the federal and state contracting policy. At federal level, the Department of Labor Employment Standards Administration (ESA) monitors compliance with the 1964 Civil Rights Act and administers the executive order 11246. The Department of Labor estimates that more than 26 per cent of the labour force in America works for federal contractors and subcontractors and is subject to compliance administered by the ESA. Examples include banks, which administer federal deposits and savings bonds. The ESA also runs equal employment opportunity and affirmative action programmes and compliance evaluations. Recipients of federal financial assistance such as work training agencies, and of technical services, are also subject to monitoring compliance with the legislation by the Office of Assistant Secretary for Administration and Management (OSBMA). The latter provides technical assistance to promote voluntary compliance with the civil rights laws. There is also an Executive Order 12677 administered by the OSBMA to increase the involvement of historically black colleges and universities in employment programmes (Department of Labor, 2000).

Employment in the public sector in the USA is also subject to the civil rights legislation. Federal and state departments have affirmative action programmes to redress under-utilisation. Federal agencies report the results of their Federal Equal Opportunity Recruitment Programme to the Office of Personnel Management, and submit annual reports of their Affirmative Action Programmes to the EEOC. The Office of Personnel Management provides guidance and training to federal agencies and also publishes detailed statistical information on black, Hispanic and Asian minorities in federal employment.

In Canada the employment equity legislation applies to government employment. Federal and state departments and local city authorities have affirmative action programmes to reduce under-utilisation of personnel from visible minorities. The Canadian Human Rights Commission[12] produces guidance for employers and monitors employers' annual reports under the Employment Equity Act.

---

12. see www.chrc.ca

South Africa adopted an affirmative action policy for the public services in 1998. All public service departments and municipalities have challenging numerical targets and time-frames within which these are to be met. The implementation of affirmative action policies is incorporated into managers' performance objectives and into the performance contracts of directors-general.[13]

Promoting diversity in education

There are two strands to the promotion of diversity in education. One is to ensure that the children from an ethnic minority background have equal opportunities and that school provision meets their needs, especially those from a disadvantaged background. The second is to ensure that the curriculum is neither biased nor mono-cultural, and promotes tolerance and an intercultural perspective.

Although the provision of equal opportunities in education for children from the ethnic minorities is essential, this paper will concentrate on the promotion of diversity through the promotion of tolerance and with an intercultural approach. Most western European governments opt for the promotion of tolerance rather than an intercultural approach, mainly on the grounds that the small proportion of ethnic or cultural minorities does not justify a true intercultural curriculum.

Europe
Norway's national curriculum guidelines for compulsory education state that schools must teach respect for others in spite of differences. There are awareness programmes aimed at school pupils to combat racism and intolerance. A textbook 'Norway as a multicultural society' has been distributed to secondary institutions to combat the limited number of secondary level textbooks dealing with cultural or racial issues. There is also a teaching programme for educational institutions 'Norway is a multi-cultural society' (Council of Europe, 2000c).

The Netherlands has a policy of promoting intercultural education and a campaign to improve the proportion of school staff with non-Dutch cultural backgrounds (Fourteenth CERD Report, 1999).

Sweden introduced an intercultural approach in education in 1985, and it is included in teacher training and in teaching resources (Perotti, 1994).

13.   see www.gov.za/structure/pubserv.html

In Britain, the recent focus has been on preventing racism in schools. A publication 'Excellence in Schools' includes guidance on tackling racial harassment and stereotyping, and in promoting a harmonious environment in which learning can flourish. The government is also amending the National Curriculum aimed at valuing diversity. Teacher training incorporates a requirement for trainees to demonstrate that they are able to set high standards for pupils regardless of cultural or linguistic background. There is provision for faith-based schools to be funded providing they deliver the National Curriculum and two Muslim schools are currently funded. Many schools adapt their uniform requirements to cater for Muslim sensitivities, provide prayer facilities and halal food (Home Office, 15th Report to CERD).

The EU is supporting a pilot project 'No racism at school' in Belgium, the Netherlands and Spain, to establish a structure for intercultural education and to promote tolerance.

Outside Europe

As in employment, in the USA the promotion of diversity in education is carried out in a framework of compliance with the civil rights laws. The Department of Education Office of Civil Rights is responsible for receiving complaints, for enforcing federal statutes against racial discrimination, and for ensuring that there is compliance by those receiving financial assistance. The Office of Civil Rights also provides technical assistance to help institutions achieve voluntary compliance. The civil rights laws cover all state education agencies and universities, and all activities (Office for Civil Rights, 1999).

Australia and Canada apply an intercultural policy to education. Canada has had a multi-cultural policy since 1971 and a Multiculturalism Act since 1988. One of its aims is to promote multiculturalism in education in partnership with educational institutions. Activities include reviewing curricula and developing resource materials for schools. Under Australia's Community Relations Strategy, priority was given to promoting positive attitudes among young people of different racial and religious backgrounds and an anti-racist resource kit has been distributed to schools.

South Africa's main priority has been to establish a non-racial education system, and to equalise educational resources, which under the former apartheid regime allocated three times as much to white pupils than to black ones. The apartheid structures had to be dismantled to produce an integrated department and teaching force. Educational policies and curriculum, training and provision were all transformed. A new curriculum was introduced to implement a non-racist learner-centred approach (Department of Education, 2001).

Monitoring and evaluating diversity

Numerous studies of the elimination of racial discrimination have commented on the need for accurate data on the ethnic composition of the population and, in employment, of the workforce (for example, ILO 1998; Coussey, 2000a; Council of Europe, 1997). This data is not available in many European countries included in this paper. Most countries use data on nationality combined with birthplace abroad, from a variety of sources such as the census, and labour or population registries (see Chapter 2, Europe's ethnic minorities).

Europe

In France the penal code makes it an offence to record data on race. Evaluation of the legislation or of measures to promote diversity tends to be done in research surveys and studies.

The Netherlands and the UK are at present the only countries in Europe to have data on the ethnic origin of the population. The UK used ethnic self-identification in the census and produces a wide range of official data from surveys with ethnicity as a key variable. Employers, local government and others use local or national census data to provide benchmarks of ethnic minority representation. The Netherlands uses birthplace and parental birthplace. These methods are used in most official surveys and provide a range of indicators of social and economic progress. Employers are required to register ethnicity to meet their obligations under the equal participation law.

Norway's Central Population Register which allocates a unique individual number to each person, links to national immigration statistics to give situational and longitudinal data on people of immigrant origin (Council of Europe, 1997).

One other measure is of public attitudes towards ethnic minorities and to diversity. Although attitude surveys give some indication over time of long-term changes, they are volatile and influenced by recent events. Different local influences and different understandings of concepts and questions affect any international comparisons which might be made. Surveys carried out by Eurobarometer (Thalhammer et al, 2001) since 1997 indicate that, in the EU, support for policies which improve community relations tends to have increased, and so has the proportion who consider that immigrants enrich a country's social and cultural life (33 per cent in 1997 to 48 per cent in 2000). But concerns about the impact of minorities on social peace and welfare have also increased.

Outside Europe

The USA has detailed census statistics on the ethnic origin of the population. The US Census Bureau publishes social and economic characteristics on race and ethnicity and has special 'Minority Links' publications on the Black/African American, Hispanic, Asian/Pacific Islander and American Indian populations . Employers use US Census Bureau labour-force data on race and job categories for preparing reports on under-utilisation for their affirmative action programmes and for contract compliance reports. This data is available at local level by state, county or city. Specialist private contractors also provide it.

Canada collects ethnic origin on the census. Ten visible minority groups were defined according to the needs of the Employment Equity Act. These are Blacks, Chinese, Filipinos, Koreans, Latin Americans, other Pacific Islanders, South Asians, South East Asians, West Asians and Arabs. Detailed information on socio-economic characteristics and the local labour-force is available from Statistics Canada.

Australia collects information in the census on birthplace, religion, language and ancestry. The latter allows Aboriginal people to be identified. The information with ethnicity indicators is available in a range of socio-economic characteristics from the Australian Bureau of Statistics.

South Africa collects data on population groups in the census. The categories are African/black, Coloured, Indian/Asian, white and other. The South African Statistics Council supplies a detailed range of socio-economic facts about population groups. Employers are required to monitor the composition of their workforce and set goals to reduce under-representation. The data is used in evaluating government policies to secure equal opportunities and the equitable distribution of resources.

Table 4: Examples of government activities to promote diversity

	Information campaigns	Public service employment	Monitoring/ evaluation	Low-level racism
Belgium	By Centre for Equality of Opportunity and Opposition to Racism and relevant ministries	Recruitment campaign to encourage ethnic minority applicants	By research projects using nationality	Centre for Equality of Opportunity and municipalities
Canada	By Federal Department of Multiculturalism and Citizenship and Human Rights Commission	Affirmative action programmes	Census and official survey data include ethnic origin.	Federal Department of Multiculturalism and Citizenship, Human Rights Commission and provincial agencies
France	By Ministry of Employment and Solidarity, ADRI, and local départements.	Nationality restrictions in public services	By research using nationality. Recording of race forbidden by Act of 1978 and Criminal Code	Departmental commissions and local mediation schemes
Germany	By Federal labour ministry and regional commissioners for foreigners	Nationality restrictions in public services	By research using nationality	In regions, offices/ commissions for foreigners, and local community centres
Netherlands	By ministries and local government	Legal obligations to achieve proportional representation	From parental birthplace records in official statistics. Annual integration monitor and research	Network of anti-discrimination centres and national bureau (LDR)
Norway	By Integration Department and local municipalities.	Action Plan to promote ethnic diversity in state administration	From Central Population Register	Local action plans in municipalities supported by ministries
South Africa	All relevant ministries	Affirmative action required	Census includes ethnic origin	Human Rights Commission
Sweden	By ministries and state agencies	Ethnic diversity campaigns in state agencies	From research using nationality	Local action plans in municipalities supported by ministries

	Information campaigns	Public service employment	Monitoring/ evaluation	Low-level racism
UK	Home Office and other key departments publish good practice and guidance. Advice and information	Diversity targets in Senior Civil Service, departmental action programmes targets, and progress reports. Annual report on race equality in public services	Census and official survey data includes ethnic origin	Local networks of Race Equality Councils, supported by local government in partnership with local agencies
USA	All relevant departments of State publish guidance on compliance	Affirmative action required	Census and official survey data includes ethnic origin	State and county level activities

7.   Conclusions

Taking the CERD provisions as the yardstick for assessing the adequacy of the measures taken in tackling racial discrimination, hate crimes and racist speech, and in promoting the benefits of diversity, it is possible to see gaps in all the countries covered in this paper.

European countries are the weakest in making specific provisions to tackle racial discrimination. Their legal arrangements are incoherent, with a mixture of civil and criminal laws, or labour codes, and a variety of enforcement mechanisms. In countries that rely on criminal codes for preventing discrimination, the law is little used because of the higher burden of proof needed. Most have no explicit provision for positive action, and some countries have no provision for individuals to bring cases. Ireland, Norway, Sweden, the Netherlands, and the UK are exceptions, as there is one civil statute (sometimes two, if employment is treated separately), and an enforcement body – although with a variety of powers and assistance available. The Netherlands and Northern Ireland also impose positive obligations on employers. Member states of the EU will, however, improve on this when the 2000 Race Discrimination Directive is implemented.

Australia, Canada and the USA have the most consistent and comprehensive civil legislation against discrimination, with specialist enforcement bodies and assistance. So too does South Africa. Canada, South Africa and the USA also have provision for affirmative action and impose positive requirements on employers. These countries, however, do not have specific regulations against hate speech.

In contrast, and undoubtedly as a result of experience of Nazism and fascism, several European countries have specific laws on hate speech and against specified groups. Many European countries too have concentrated their efforts into promoting the benefits of immigration and diversity, and into encouraging tolerance. However, there is confusion about terminology and difficulties about obtaining factual data to identify differences of access and to monitor progress. This reflects their relatively recent experiences of immigration and ethnic diversity. The exceptions again are mainly Britain and the Netherlands, which have the longest experience of implementing policies to prevent racism and discrimination and to promote diversity.

How effective are the different legal measures against discrimination and hate crimes, and also measures to promote diversity? The ILO has carried out the only major attempt to make international comparisons, using standardised methodology to document levels of discrimination, but the work was confined to employment.

The ILO concluded that comprehensive civil legislation is more effective than reliance on penal codes, and that mandatory monitoring and requirements to adopt positive action were indispensable. The ILO also concluded that a combination of legal, organisational, administrative and political/educational measures was required. A country with all such measures may expect to see improvements in the social and economic position of people from the ethnic minorities.

In Britain and the Netherlands, countries with the most comprehensive approaches in Europe, there are signs of improvements. For example, in the Netherlands, ethnic minority people have improved their overall employment rates, especially young people from the second generation, and there has also been an overall improvement in employment levels.

Britain can also show improvements in educational attainment and employment levels among people from particular ethnic groups, for example, of Indian and Chinese origins (Department for Education and Employment, 2000). Britain has a relatively high rate of mixed partnerships especially of Caribbeans, one in five of whom has a white partner (Modood et al., 1997).

The USA too, which has the strongest emphasis on regulation, can show improvements in the proportion of minorities with higher education and in managerial and professional positions (US Census Bureau, 2000). There is also a growing proportion of mixed partnerships, and according to the US Census, one third of young people aged under 18 are multiethnic – that is, of more than one race.

Bertaux et al. (1996) *Roles et perspectives des femmes relais en France.* Paris: ADRI.

Bendick, M. (1996) *Discrimination against racial/ethnic minorities in access to employment in the United State.* Geneva: ILO.

Bendick, M. Jr et al. (1998) *The documentation and evaluation of anti-discrimination training in the United States.* Geneva: ILO.

Bjorgo, T and Witte, R. (1993) *Racist Violence in Europe.* Basingstoke: Macmillan

Brouillet, J et al. (Eds.) (1999) *Guide practique pour reussir la diversite culturelle en enterprise.* Vernouillet: MRH.

Bureau voor Economische Argumetatie (1994) *De economische betekenis van minderheden voor de arbeidsmarkt.* Hoofddorp: BEA.

Clancy et al. (2001) *Crime, Policing and Justice: the experience of ethnic minorities. Findings from the 2001 British Crime Survey.* Home Office Research Study 223. London: Home Office.

Council of Europe (1994) *Police training concerning migrants and ethnic relations.* Strasbourg: Council of Europe Publishing.

Council of Europe (1995) *Tackling racism and xenophobia.* Strasbourg: Council of Europe Publishing.

Council of Europe (1997) *Measures and indicators of integration.* Strasbourg: Council of Europe Publishing.

Council of Europe (1998) *The situation of Roma/Gypsies in Economic and Employment Field in Europe.* Strasbourg: Council of Europe Publishing.

Council of Europe (1999) *Exchange of experience on recruitment and employment initiatives for immigrants/ethnic minorities in the public service.* Strasbourg: Council of Europe Publishing.

Council of Europe (2000) *Diversity and Cohesion*. Strasbourg: Council of Europe Publishing.

Council of Europe (2000a) *Strategies for Implementing Integration Policies*. Strasbourg: Council of Europe Publishing.

Council of Europe (2000b) *Training and guidance Memorandum on Equal Opportunities for Staff in Employment Services working with disadvantaged communities*. Strasbourg: Council of Europe Publishing.

Council of Europe, ECRI. (2000c) *Second Report on Norway*. Strasbourg: Council of Europe Publishing.

Council of Europe, ECRI. (1998a) *Legal measures to combat racism and intolerance in the member states of the Council of Europe*. Strasbourg: Council of Europe Publishing.

Council of Europe, ECRI. (1998b) *Country by Country approach: Volume II*. Strasbourg: Council of Europe Publishing.

Coussey, M. (2000a) *Framework of Integration Policies*. Strasbourg: Council of Europe Publishing.

Coussey, M. (2000b) *The role of the employment services in the promotion of equal opportunities for immigrants and people from disadvantaged ethnic minority groups*. Strasbourg: Council of Europe publishing.

Cowl, T. (1995) *Responding to Hate*. Department of Canadian Heritage.

De Santis, H. (1998) *Combating Hate on the Internet*. Department of Canadian Heritage.

Pathak, S. (March 2000) *Department for Education and Employment. `Ethnicity in Education, Training and the Labour Market*. Research Topic Paper. London: DfEE.

Department of Education (2001) *Education in South Africa: Achievements since 1994*. http://education.pwv.gov.za/Policies-Reports/reports-2001/education-in-south-africa.

Department of Justice (1996) *Complaint and Redress Mechanisms relation to Racial Discrimination*. Canada.

Department of Labor Annual Report (2000):www.dol.gov/dol-sec/public/media/reports/annual2000

European Commission against Racism and Intolerance [ECRI] (1997) *General Policy Recommendations Nos. 1 and 2.* Strasbourg: Council of Europe Publishing.

European Monitoring Centre on Racism and Xenophobia (1998) *Looking Reality in the Face.* Vienna: EUMC.

Eurostat (1995) *Migration Statistics.* Luxembourg: Statistical Office of the European Communities.

Federal Register Title 29 Chapter XIV Part 1607 (1978). *Uniform Guidelines on Employee Selection Procedures.*

Fitzgerald, M et al. (1996) *Ethnic minorities: victimisation and racial harassment.* Home Office Research Study 154. London: Home Office.

Fourteenth periodic report of the Netherlands to the UN Committee on the Elimination of Racial Discrimination (1999). Geneva: CERD.

Glover, S. et al. (2001) *Migration: an economic and social analysis.* Home Office RDS Occasional Paper No. 67: London: Home Office.

Guild, E. Ed. (1999) *The Legal Framework and Social Consequences of Free Movement of Persons in the European Union.* Boston: Kluwer Law International.

Hepple B. et al. (2000) *Equality: A New Framework.* Oxford: Hart Publishing.

Home Office (2000a) *Statistics on Race and the Criminal Justice System.* London: Home Office.

Home Office (2000b) *Race equality in public services.* London: Home Office.

Home Office (2001a) *Race equality in public services.* London: Home Office.

Home Office (2001b) *Race Relations (Amendment) Act 2000. New Laws for a Successful Multi-Racial Britain.* London: Home Office.

Home Office *15th Periodic Report to the UN Committee on the Elimination of All Forms of Racial Discrimination.* London: Home Office.

ILO (1998) *A Manual on Achieving Equality for Migrant and Ethnic Minority Workers.* Geneva: ILO.

ILO (2000) *A Manual on Achieving Equality for Migrant and Ethnic Minority Workers.* Geneva: ILO.

Martens, E. et al. (2000) *Integration Monitor 2000.* Rotterdam: Institute for Sociological-Economic Research.

Mattison, J. et al. (2000) *Attitudes to Crime and Criminal Justice.* Home Office Research Study 200. London: Home Office.

McIntosh N; Smith D. (1974) *The Extent of Racial Discrimination.* Political and Economic Planning Broadsheet.

Modood, T. and Berthoud, R. (1997) *Ethnic Minorities in Britain.* London: Policy Studies Institute.

Oakley, R. (1996) *Tackling racist and xenophobic violence in Europe: Review and Practical Guidance'.* Strasbourg: Council of Europe Publishing.

Oakley, R. (1997) *Tackling racist and xenophobic violence in Europe: Case Studies.* Strasbourg: Council of Europe Publishing.

OECD (1999) *Trends in International Migration.* SOPEMI 1999. Paris: OECD.

Office for Civil Rights, US Department of Education (1999) *The Impact of Civil Rights Laws.* www.ed.gov/offices/ORC/impact.html 1999.

Perotti, A. (1994) *The case for intercultural education.* Strasbourg: Council of Europe Publishing.

Report by Denmark to the UN Committee on the Elimination of Racial Discrimination (2000). Geneva: CERD.

Sibbitt, R. (1997) *The perpetrators of racial harassment and racial violence.'* Home Office Research Study 176. London: Home Office.

Talhammer, E, et al. (2001) *Attitudes towards minority groups in the European Union*. SORA, Vienna, for the European Monitoring Centre on Racism and Xenophobia.

Tribalat, M. et al. (1991) *Cent Ans d'Immigration, Etrangers d'Hier, Francais d'Aujourd'hui*. Paris: INED.

US Census Bureau (March 2000) *Black Population in the US*.

US Department of Labor (1988) *Opportunity 2000*. Washington.

Ventura, C. (1995) *From outlawing discrimination to promoting equality: Canada's experience with anti-discrimination legislation*. Geneva: ILO.

Wrench, J, et al. (1993) *A research manual on the evaluation of anti-discrimination training activities*. Geneva: ILO.

Zegers de Beijl R. Ed. (Undated) *Migrant Discrimination in the Labour Market*. Geneva: ILO.

RDS Publications

Requests for Publications

Copies of our publications and a list of those currently available may be obtained from:

> Home Office
> Research, Development and Statistics Directorate
> Communication Development Unit
> Room 275, Home Office
> 50 Queen Anne's Gate
> London SW1H 9AT
> Telephone: 020 7273 2084 (answerphone outside of office hours)
> Facsimile: 020 7222 0211
> E-mail: publications.rds@homeoffice.gsi.gov.uk

alternatively

why not visit the RDS website at
> Internet: http://www.homeoffice.gov.uk/rds/index.html

where many of our publications are available to be read on screen or downloaded for printing.